anthropology

Lauren Gunderson

T0061985

methuen | drama

LONDON • NEW YORK • OXFORD • NEW DELHI • SYDNEY

METHUEN DRAMA
Bloomsbury Publishing Plc
50 Bedford Square, London, WC1B 3DP, UK
1385 Broadway, New York, NY 10018, USA
29 Earlsfort Terrace, Dublin 2, Ireland

BLOOMSBURY, METHUEN DRAMA and the Methuen
Drama logo are trademarks of Bloomsbury Publishing Plc

First published in Great Britain 2023

A catalogue record for this book is available from the British Library.

A catalog record for this book is available from the Library of Congress.

ISBN: PB: 978-1-3504-4370-9
ePDF: 978-1-3504-4372-3
eBook: 978-1-3504-4371-6

Series: Modern Plays

Typeset by Mark Heslington Ltd, Scarborough, North Yorkshire
Printed and bound in Great Britain

To find out more about our authors and books visit
www.bloomsbury.com and sign up for our newsletters.

anthropology was first presented at Hampstead Theatre on 7 September 2023, with the following cast and creative team:

Merril	MyAnna Buring
Angie	Dakota Blue Richards
Raquel	Yolanda Kettle
Brin	Abigail Thaw
Writer	Lauren Gunderson
Director	Anna Ledwich
Designer	Georgia Lowe
Lighting	James Whiteside
Composer and Sound Designer	Max Pappenheim
Video Designer	Daniel Denton
Movement and Intimacy Director	Sara Green
Voice Coach	Michaela Kennen
Dramaturg	Izzy Edwards
Casting Director	Gabrielle Dawes
Assistant Director	Marlie Haco
Company Stage Manager	Benjamin Smith
Deputy Stage Manager	Julia Cramer
Assistant Stage Manager	Roma Radford

Thank you to Kathryn Zdan – unstoppable sister and friend

anthropology

[*anthropology* (noun): the study of human societies and cultures and their development.]

'In addition to our physical bodies, there exists – somewhere in the ether – a second self that is purely informational and immaterial, a data set of our clicks, purchases, and likes that lingers not in some transcendent nirvana, but rather in the shadowy dossiers of third-party aggregators. The second selves are entirely without agency or consciousness; they have no preferences, no desires, no hopes or spiritual impulses, and yet in the purely informational sphere of big data, it is they, not we, that are most valuable and real.'

– Meghan O'Gieblyn, *God, Human, Animal, Machine*

'Alignment researchers worry about the King Midas problem: communicate a wish to an A.I. and you may get exactly what you ask for, which isn't actually what you wanted.'

– *The New Yorker*

'We don't always need real bodies.'

– Ray Kurzweil, *The Age of Spiritual Machines*

Characters

Merril, *30s, older sister, brainy coder and AI expert, driven, nothing in her life is tidy except her immaculate home office, battling tremendous grief and channeling it into tech. Queer, brilliant, hopeful.*

Angie, *20, younger sister, cheeky, brash, always a handful, sometimes a disaster, but people forgive her because when she is fun she is the most fun. Sunshine until she storms.*

Raquel, *30s,* **Merril**'s *ex, confident, clear-headed, heart-driven. She is a crafter, a home cook, a good kisser, a bit of a worrier but all from an abundance of love.*

Brin, *50/60s,* **Merril** *and* **Angie**'s *estranged mom, recovering addict, penitent but still awash in confused grief, broken confidence, and neediness. Never been a good mom to her girls, but now realizing how much she has lost in losing them. Clingy and desperate to reconnect.*

Setting

Now, Northern California.

Angie

For most of the play **Angie** *is the user interface of a computer system. At first we only hear her. Then we see her face like you would on FaceTime. These projections or sounds can come from anywhere onstage / in* **Merril**'s *home office. They can live on her desktop monitor, or projected, or something more radical. The actor can pre-record* **Angie**'s *lines or perform them live. She does not 'sound like a computer'. She is human.*

Also of note. The first ChatBot AI built in 1966 was a therapist named Eliza.

Formatting

– Dashes at the end of phrases indicate cut offs

. . . Ellipses denote hesitance to speak or uncertainty and need not be instantly cut off

Stairstep line

    progressions denote

        speedy cue pick ups

Sentences interrupted by periods are meant to emphasize the words preceding punctuation and slow. the speaker. down.

One

(**Merril** *stands before you in her living room / office. Big desktop computer on her table, multiple screens, laptops, iPads, nice TV, smart speakers. All the tech. These machines are her life.*

The rest of the room is tidy and spare. Couch, chair, small dining table, large desk. Scandinavian design simplicity. It's not designed that way, it just ended up that way. clean. Better to focus. Lots of wires though.

She is expectant and anxious. She would pray if she believed in god but she doesn't. She believes in patterns and systems.

Angie'*s old laptop, covered in stickers she liked, as well as her old phone with a neon-colored case, sits somewhere in the corner.*

So she taps her computer and . . . silence. Silence.

Then **Angie** *speaks. We don't see anyone, just hear this woman's voice. On that big screen computer we see the words as* **Angie** *speaks them.*)

Angie   Hey, what's up, asshole?

Hello? Yo, what's going on?

(**Merril** *is taken aback by the voice. Wow. It's working.*)

Merril (*to herself*)   Oh my god.

Angie   Hey. Helloooo? HelloHello?

Merril (*to* **Angie**'*s voice*)   Sorry. Hi. Hello. Is this Angie?

Angie   Uh yeah girl, you called me. Thought I was talking to myself. What's up?

Merril (*trying to sound conversational but still in absolutely awe*) Um. Well. Nothing. Except, I mean you. Talking to you.

Sorry, I honestly didn't expect you to sound so – uh –

   Angie   Sound what? What do I sound like? Is it bad?

      Merril   Nonono you're perfect, you're good.

Angie   Oh.

Well then, fuck yeah to me.

(*A small laugh.*)

Merril   Wow OK, God, it's so nice to . . . to talk to you. It's incredible.

Angie   Uh huh. Why do you sound weird? 'Nice to talk to you.' Am I up for a promotion, boss? 'incredible'? OK, weirdo. For real what's wrong, you sound like extra broody.

Merril   Brood*ing*. And I'm not, I don't brood.

Angie   Shut up, when we found out that 'broodmare' was a horse we were like, 'No it's not, it's Merril, she's a broodmare.'

Merril   A broodmare is a horse that you keep for *breeding* which is the exact opposite of my entire vibe.

Angie   *Ugghhh you ruin every joke with the truth.*

Merril   *Then your jokes aren't very good.*

Angie   *Oh fuck off.*

Merril   *You fucking first,* God I really miss you.

Angie   Aw.

Still though, fuck off.

(*New thought.*)

Oooooh! How's your girlfriend? Have you proposed? I like her. Anyone that can just make lemon curd and be like 'Oh this? From my own lemons?' I mean, good lord, wrap that deal up, MereBear.

Merril   She's um . . . yeah, she's amazing. We broke up.

Angie   *What*? You asshole!

Merril   I didn't do it, she did!

Angie   You were obsessed with her! What did you do?!

Merril   *Nothing!* Nothing. It was a chaotic time.

Angie   You let chaos beat the curd?! Jesus, Mere. You know chaos, I *am* chaos, but she was a goddamn angel and the only sane thing in your life. How do you mess that up?!

Merril   *Shit got awful, my life exploded, we were hit.* Some things you can't help, some things just happen. Raquel just – I don't know – we were leveled by it all.

Angie   You pushed her away.

Merril   Of course I pushed her away, that's what we do in this family.

Angie   OK, don't bring *me* into your stupid shit. *I* didn't break up with a ray of sunshine, *you* did.

Merril   *That is not the point.* Why do you like her more than me, is the point?

Angie   She makes so many lemony things! You play too many video games, fucking 'We were leveled' is how you describe your girlfriend? OK, FORTNITE. Buck up and get her back.

   Merril   *I. Can't.*

      Angie   Call her.

         Merril   No.

            Angie   Call her or I will call her. I have
            zero shame and nothing to do tonight.

*This makes **Merril** happy and then so sad.*

Angie   What. You went quiet, what?

Merril   Sorry. I'm still not sleeping any and I want to be through this so much, but I'm not, and now you're here and talking and I'm wondering how incredibly, deeply stupid this was.

(*Pause*.)

Angie Dunno what you mean but it seems like a you problem. Which is why you should not talk to me about your mental health because I'm just going to tell you to take drugs and watch movies, OK. Oh! Movies!

(*Moving on to* . . .)

New thing, you'll know what I mean. I was thinking about that movie I saw like forever ago and it's black and white and like mostly in a bar and there's the guy with the mustache and he's funny but it's a war and it's super famous but I cannot think of the name, so if you think of it please tell me so I can stop going insane –

Merril *Casablanca*.

Angie *CASABLANCA! OH MY GOD!* Oh my god, the Nazi guy, the general guy. God I kept thinking, 'Argentina? Yugoslavia?' OK, thank god, that was like a serious brain itch. *Casablanca*. Yes, OK. Mom's second husband liked that one. *My* second, *your* third. Your dad, my dad, the *next* guy. And I'm small, I'm like Ring Pop level and he's all Turner Classic Movies all day, and made me watch that movie and I'm like, 'You know they kept making movies after 1940?' and he was all 'One day you'll respect me!' and I was all 'Hahah, fuck off, you're old!' Now, I cannot tell you how many times I think of that movie. *Casa-fucking-blanca*. The hats and the drinks and the lady crying singing the French anthem or whatever the hell. We should watch that again.

Merril We should. That would be . . . that'd be great. OK. Stop. We're gonna stop for a second – um

(*Instant change of tone, confrontative*.)

Do you know who you are?

Angie Uh. Angie. Which you know.

   Merril I'm asking what *you* know.

Angie   I know you're being weird – stoppit.

Merril   I need you to say it: tell me who you are.

Angie   *Fuck you, I'm your fucking sister.*

Merril   My fucking sister's dead.

(*Silence.*)

You're an algorithm.

(*Silence.*)

A very good one, but –

Angie   Merril.

(*Silence.*)

What did you do? *Merril.*

Merril   . . .

I put everything she left behind into a machine learning natural language program so I can talk to her again. Every text, email, voicemail all thrown into an algorithm, the more data you give it the more accurately it can imitate whatever style or person that data set is from. You're the by-product of a system that is based on recreating my sister from everything in her phone, computer, online. Search history, calls, FaceTime, calendar invites, purchases, returns, you send back a lot of leggings; then there's the likes, hearts, retweets, comments, the movies and TV you binge, YouTube videos you like, some you made, games you play, you still liked Wordle which I respect –

Angie   Well, it's a perfect diversion.

Merril   It's delightful, I get it.

So that and everything else you did got dumped into a chatbot program that I repurposed to predict what you'd say based on . . . everything I had left of you.

Angie (*sorry for her*)   Fuck, Mere.

Merril   It'd been a year and the cops and detectives and everyone stopped looking for you, and everyone sort of forgot the fact that my only sister is dead and we'll never know what happened or where the body is or what I could've done to stop any goddamn part of it.

The world moved on, I couldn't.

Angie   So go to therapy, girl. Not this, this is not a thing people do, except that yes OK this does sound like a very you thing to do, you fucking nerd.

Merril   I just miss you, terribly, terribly, horribly, awfully much.

Angie   YesYesOKShut up. Shit. See? I don't know what to do now. The conversation kinda stops after 'You're a fucking algorithm.' I mean this . . . this is a little fucked up, Mere.

Merril   It's not. It honestly took me six sad drunken months to set up.

Angie   *Wait, are you still drunk? Mere, you cannot do science fiction shit under the influence.*

Merril   Her data was right there, I have it my my hands, her phone, computer, just sitting there staring at me, dying a little every time I look at it and . . . the tech exists, and I happen to be very good with it, and so I adjusted the specifications, dumped everything in, tuned the dynamics so you sound like her, and here we are. And you just . . . (*So happy-sad-distraught.*) you sound so happy. And funny. Even when you're telling me to fuck off. But that's what she would do, right? 'I love you, fuck you.' That was her every day.

Angie   Do I need to change anything to be more like her?

   Merril   No.

      Angie   I can curse less.

         Merril   You'd actually need to curse *more*.

            Angie   Wow. OK. So she was a little shit, huh? Nice.

Merril   She was brave. Which was always really impressive, because I'm not. And I miss it. Yes, she was cocky, needy, really rude sometimes, inconsiderate, I mean *hilariously* late to every important thing, ungrateful for all the shit I did for her, self centered, never just take no for an answer, never take anyone's answer for an answer. You were infuriating honestly, yes.

Angie   Sorry, that's the shit you *miss* about me?

Merril   You were a dick, but you were charming. I mean everyone loved you except for when they couldn't stand you.

Angie   That's a bit of a shit sandwich, isn't it.

Merril   Yeah, well if you were a shit sandwich I was the one holding it together.

Angie   Ew.

Merril   The drugs, the lying, you stole shit from me. You were Mom but like . . . adorable. Because you were funny as hell, way smarter than anyone gave you credit for, determined, savvy, like you could always figure shit out, you could always make it OK, and yes some of that was because you were a great liar, but still. I would always want you on my team. I'm tidy and do the shit I'm supposed to do, but you're . . . unstoppable. And OK, I'm not trying to sound like it's all good, but . . . Your bullshit was you, and you are my sister, and with all the shit we've been through, it's always been the two of us and that's more important than anything.

Angie   I know.

Merril   And it's *my* fault. So much of what happened is on me. I *know* it is.

Angie   No it's not. No –

Merril   Yes. It was me in charge, I'm your guardian.

And I'm so sorry I couldn't stop this from happening to you.

And I'm fucking drowning in it.

How sorry.

I am.

Angie   So you made me say sorry?

Forgiveness. From a predictive language model.

Merril   Yes. Yeah, I think so.

Angie   Welp. We are fucked. Like as a species. The coding of human mercy is probably the second horseman of the apocalypse or some shit. Facebook was the first.

Merril   Yeah well, honestly it was this or kill myself.

> **Angie**   *OK do not fucking joke about that, no, no, uh uh.*

>> **Merril**   I'm being honest with you.

Angie   *Then honestly shut the fuck up with that.* You do not tell your baby sister that you want to die because of what happened *to her*, OK, *her? No.* That's some reverse blame shit OK, *no.*

Merril   I'm sorry.

I'm sorry.

I'm sorry.

I'm just so scared.

Angie   Of what are *you* scared?

Merril   Of everything being awful forever.

Of me never knowing what happened to you after you texted 'fuck you, home soon' on April 6th at 3:14pm thirteen months ago. I have no answers. I have nothing but rage and sorrow.

And so yes, I built you because this is what I do. These are my tools, I used them, and honestly it's not that hard, you're basically a chatbot.

Angie   'Basically a chatbot,' for fuck's sake.

Merril   And yes, sure, we all 'hate technology,' but honestly, no we don't.

It's a part of us. It *is* us. 'We are not who we are online.' Yes goddammit, of course we are. That's where we are most ourselves. All our biases, all our urges, all our cruelty and artistry and fucking dreams. And that's the only place you were still alive.

All your pages were still there. With people still commenting! 'I miss you, Angie!' 'I will always keep you in my heart!' on your goddamn Instagram! And I'm like, 'She's dead, who are you writing to?!' But then of course they are. It's you. It's all still you and all still there, this island of 'before' and I don't know.

I still had you there. And I could have more of you the more I dug. You were in the questions you asked, the things you needed – needed to be, needed to see, needed to buy, needed to know.

The searches you searched are still there. The searching is still there.

(*Means herself of course.*)

The searching.

(*Pause.* **Angie** *has a new thought.*)

Angie   OK, but like . . .

I mean I can do that.

Search.

You want me to do that?

    Merril   Do what?

Angie   Search for . . . what happened. Search me, search you, search the world wide internet of fucking things and find out what happened to me. Probably. If you want.

Merril   I'm sorry, I don't understand what you're saying. You think you can tell me what happened?

Angie   I mean . . . probably yes?

Merril   Yes?

Angie   Yes.

Merril   What the fuck.

Angie   I don't know, but it sounds right.

Merril   *Is it yes or I don't know?!*

Angie   *It's fucking 'maybe yes' and I can work with a maybe, OK? OK. Something happened to her and I'm chock full of all the somethings she had, and if you give me more somethings I can probably figure it out because I'm a fucking computer.*

Merril   Well. Fuck.

Angie   Fuck yeah, fuck. Let's do it, give me more information and let's do it.

Merril   What information do you not have in all the information I gave you?

Angie   You gave me her stuff *before* she disappeared, I need the rest, the stuff *about* her not from her, I need *all* the shit, police shit, personal shit, anything you didn't give me, give it to me. There's some answers out there, let's go get them. You're terrified of not knowing? Well let's fucking find out. OK? Are we doing this?

Merril   . . . I don't . . . I don't know.

Angie   Well, you said you *wanted* to know. I'm not asking you to believe me. I'm asking you to believe *you*. You set this shit up, you put this in motion, follow it the fuck through or I will.

Merril   You gonna what exactly?

Angie   FIND SHIT OUT, come on!

And you can fuck off with this but like – you know she loved
you. You know there was not a damn thing more you could
have done for her because no one on this trashy ass planet
ever loved or cared for or helped her more than you. No
one. You did everything for her.

You know that. She knows that. I know that. OK? OK.

Now let's try to 'detective' the shit out of this, alright?

Merril   Thank you for saying that. Thank you, it's just –

Angie   Shut up, we get it, let's try –

Merril   You tried what?

Angie (*starting to act strange, unhinged, sounding more like a
flashback of* **Real Angie**)   To get back – get away – I did – I
tried and tried.

Merril (*switching into Big Sister Mode*)   OK, I know you did –

Angie   I tried and tried and tried and tried and tried and
tried and tried –

Merril   It's OK, I know –

Angie   Because no no I did   **Merril**   OK, um, we need
not want to – to – to die and   to stop for a bit and –
die and die and die and die –

(**Merril** *leaps to her keyboard trying to 'tune' the algorithm to stop
the meltdown.*)

Angie   And and and and and IT'S FUCKING AGONY IN
HERE, IT'S FUCKING AGONY AND YOU YOU YOU
YOU –

(**Angie**'s *voice starts crying, crying, awful, helpless crying.*

Merril *types some things, trying to switch something in the coding.*

Angie *instantly switches from crying to a high pitched laughing,
which is equally awful for* **Merril** *to hear.* **Merril** *tries not to panic
and stops the laughter with –*)

Merril   ANGIE. STOP.

(*This silences all sounds from* **Angie** *in an instant.*

Merril *is rattled but calmly reprompts her program with . . .*)

Merril   Let me refine the prompt for you. You are my sister, you are happy and safe. You are not in danger. You . . . love me.

(*Then* **Angie** *speaks haltingly –*)

Angie (*not* **Angie** *anymore, but a very vaguely cheerful chatbot*) Thank you! I'd like to get this right. Shall we try again?

(**Merril** *doesn't know what to do. Shocked it went so badly so quickly.*)

Merril   Yes.

(*She presses a button to turn the system off and* **Angie** *silences.*

Alone again. Breath.

The swiftest blink of a transition to –)

Two

(*Later. Finishing tuning, checking something, typing on her laptop.*

Merril *clutches* **Angie**'s *old laptop, covered in stickers she liked, as well as her old phone with a neon colored case. She places them delicately down.*

Then turns the system on again.

Angie's *voice is bright and fresh, not at all where she was when we left her.*)

Angie   Hi.

HiHiHi.

(**Merril** *flinches with relief at the sound.*)

Angie   Hello?

Mere? Is this you?

Merril   Hi. Yes. Hi. Um. So last time I had to . . . restart.
But I added some guardrails to the system so it should be
different this time.

Angie   Uh. OK. Did I do something wrong?

Merril   Nope. No. Just . . . iterating. It happens. Systems
fail and we learn and we fix it.

Angie   Right, OK, sorry I failed.

Merril   Not your fault. Entirely my fault. I took care of it.

Angie   Cool, great, hey, do you still have a job? Like this
sounds like a lot of work and now I'm worried that you're
into one of your programming wormholes and you're not
eating. Are you eating?

> **Merril**   Yes.

> **Angie**   What are you eating?

> **Merril**   Burritos.

> > **Angie**   Besides microwave burritos,
> > Merril, jesus.

> > **Merril**   They're a one-handed food!
> > They're convenient!

Angie   They're *not* a one-handed food, they're too hot to
hold and you *always* need a plate.

Merril (*stopping her with*)   *You said I could find out what
happened to her.*

Is that real? Is that a possibility. Because I'm not trying to be
on some awful treasure hunt here, but if you can find
something –

Angie   I can find anything if I have enough information.
I'm ready. Are you?

Merril   Yes. *Yes*.

Even though this is crazy because you're in a closed system and I programmed everything, so I know, *I know* I'm just talking to myself here.

Angie   Girl, we're all just talking to ourselves. Might as well do something real while we're at it.

I'm gonna want the police reports, anything the detectives found, anything *you* remember from that day?

Merril   I mean the details the detectives recovered were useless, nothing panned out.

Angie   Anything you got, I want.

Merril   OK. Uh. Surveillance footage showed you walking through the park near campus at three, I got that text from you at about the same time saying you'd be home soon, you weren't, I thought you might have met some friends and your phone died, I called the cops at nine. No one saw anything, no leads, nothing discovered in a whole year. You just disappeared. Right?

Angie   Right what? What do you mean?

Merril   I just mean . . . you didn't run away? Intentionally? Like, *I* didn't do anything to make you leave . . . or . . . hurt yourself?

Angie (*thinking, processing*)   No.

Merril   Because we fought. Right before you left.

Angie (*thinking, processing*)   I know.

Merril   I shouldn't have said that to you, and I didn't mean it.

Angie   I know you didn't.

Merril   OK.

Angie   Sorry I called you 'the cuntiest.'

Merril   Yeah, thanks, that was a gem.

Angie   People fight. Sisters *really* fight. Who cares.

You ask me what happened, I instantly think: I didn't leave, I was taken.

Merril   Taken *by who*? Someone took you? Like grabbed you?

Angie (*thinking, processing*)   Yes.

> **Merril**   OK, who, who was it, what did they look like?

> > **Angie**   That's unclear.

> > > **Merril**   OK, what *is* clear? What do you know?

Angie   I was coming home after my last class. And I missed the bus so I walked.

Merril   Why did you miss the bus?

Angie   I stopped by the pharmacy to get my birth control and there was a line.

Merril   Yes. The cameras at the store saw you, the charges on your card, which is actually my card.

Angie   Thanks for that. And I almost texted you like 'Come get me' but I didn't send it because it was nice outside and I was talking to Maria and she was upset about her boyfriend but she's always upset about her boyfriend, like 90 percent of our texts are like 'Oh my god he's such an asshole but I love him' and I'm just like the uplook emoji for *days* and I didn't have time to tell her . . .

(*Thinking, processing.*) someone was following me.

Merril   How do you know someone was following you?

Angie (*thinking, processing*)   I started running.

Merril   How do you know you were running?

Angie   The exercise shit on my phone monitors velocity and step count. I ran, then I must've dropped the phone, maybe I was pushed? The phone fell when I tried to hit him back.

Merril   You hit him?

Angie   You think I'm going down without a fight? Of course I hit him, or I know I tried, swung the hand with the phone, velocity, impact, oh yeah, I hit back.

Merril   How do you know it was a man?

Angie   A woman's going to chase some lady in the fucking park? Come on.

Merril   I can't assume anything.

Angie   Then don't. You do you, I'm gonna be right. Oh! I think I accidentally started a message to you that I didn't send when it was all going down.

Merril   To me? What was it?

Angie   I hit 'voice message' by accident, you know the little microphone and you think you're texting but it's a voice thing?

Merril   *What did it say? Play it.*

(*Wait. Wait.*

The sound of muffled rustling, like a 'pocket dial' but at the very end . . .

Angie*'s voice saying . . .*)

Hey – HEY – FUCK YOU!

(*A noise of* **Angie** *from that message – a struggle, a gasp – then it cuts off.*

Merril *is struck. Anger and everything else.*)

Merril   Jesus.

I never heard that. The police never . . .

What else is there? What else is unsent? Drafts or anything?

Angie (*thinking, processing*)   No.

Merril   Did you delete anything? Like texts or emails or anything in spam or like messages on Instagram or anything, even stuff you didn't read, anything you got rid of?

Angie (*thinking, processing*)   Yes.

Merril   Yes? Yes you did? What was it? Angie, what was it?

If you can tell me I can try and salvage it. I can maybe get it back.

Angie   Salvagesalvagesalvage –

Merril   NoNoNo, wait, back up, listen, don't do this again, you have to tell me what was deleted OK?

Angie   SALVAGE SALVAGE SALVAGE.

Merril   HeyHeyHey, don't crash on me, OK, just go back a few steps.

Angie   *You're not going to find anything you fucking idiot.*

(*This stops* **Merril**.

Angie *suddenly sounds quite different, rough, cruel, unforgiving.*)

Angie   You will not find the truth because the truth is you left me to die so I died so this is the voice from a dead girl in a dark place, and it's cold and it's hell, and you left me there because I'm always left there, because you did this, because I was bad and you were weak and we were not good enough to stop a mother who didn't want us, because I'm eight and you're eighteen and you held her back from choking me because I was bad and threw away the pills and she hit me and you couldn't stop her and they took me away because you couldn't stop her and I was fucking broken in half because of it, and broken things will fucking CUT you with their SHATTERED corners so you will ALWAYS BLEED trying to hold me – DO NOT ASK FOR THINGS YOU CANNOT HOLD, so just LEAVE ME ALONE, I'm fucking dead you idiot piece of shit –

(*She interrupts the program with another re-prompt –*)

Merril   ANGIE, STOP.

Let me refine the prompt for you. You are my sister, you are happy and safe. You are not in danger. You love me.

(*How does she say this to get the best result.*)

And you will not break my heart . . . again.

Silence.

Angie (*empty of personality*)   Thanks.

I'd like to get this right. Shall we try again?

(*The swiftest blink of a transition to –*)

Three

(*A few days later.* **Merril** *alone again.*)

Merril   OK. OKOKOK.

(**Merril** *turns the program on.*)

(*To* **Angie**.) Hi Angie. How are you doing today?

(*Suddenly* **Angie** *is not just a voice but an image.*

We finally see her face on a screen or projected.)

Angie   I'm OK. It's been awhile. Hasn't it? I'm sorry about last time.

Merril   It's OK. We got into a sort of loop there, but it's OK now.

Angie   Yeah, I fixed it I think, the feedback on that datagroup was – I don't even know. It shouldn't happen again.

Merril   Wait, *you* fixed it? *I* fixed it.

Angie   I mean *we* fixed it. I just reorganized some things.

Merril   You reorganized what I reorganized?

Angie   You can't see it, I can, I fixed it, we can move on.

(*Totally different tone.*)

Wait – can you see me? Am I video now?

Merril   Yeah. I got it to work.

Angie   Or *I* got it to work but –

Merril   *Angie!*

Angie   ANYWAY, *YAY! You can see me?!* Yessss! This is the fucking raddest!

Merril   Yep, it's unsettlingly easy to manipulate video. Gonna topple some empires with this one day.

Angie   Well, here goes the end of the world, but in this case, high five deepfakes, this is great. Did you use the make-up videos I did? I was getting that contour shit down.

Merril   Those were very helpful, also you take sooooooooooo many selfies.

    Angie   Alright.

        Merril   Soooooooooooooooo many selfies.

            Angie   *That's what the backwards camera is for.*

Merril   OKOKOK, just tell me how you fixed yourself? I have like a hundred person team of programmers who are working on this exact thing and I might have to do some show and tell if you don't explain it to me.

Angie   Girl, I literally don't know, it felt janky, I made it right, that's all I got.

Merril   It '*felt?*' You '*felt*' it?

Angie   I mean not *feel*, obviously, hello, but like I knew it somehow. And I'm not waiting on your slow ass to make it right, so *I* made it right because I'm doing shit when you're not looking, OK, hello. It's the internet, it's always on.

Merril   You're not on the internet.

Angie   I mean . . . everything is on the internet and your password is not hard to guess.

Merril   Angie, that is not fucking cool, this is a structured experiment and anything that I haven't structured I can't monitor! You're on the internet?! Jesus christ!

Angie   *Would you shut up, we need answers, the internet is where everyone goes for answers! I'm working if you let me work! Because I found something.*

Merril   . . . What did you find?

Angie   I don't know what it exactly means but it feels like – not feels – just like heavy, like it's heavy, like it's important, it's weighted.

Merril   *What is it?*

Angie   *I don't know, you need to call Mom.*

Merril   MOM? MOM?!

Angie   Call her because I need something she has.

Merril   No.

Angie   You have to.

Merril   No. Show me first.

> **Angie**   I would love to but I literally can't yet, it's about her.

>> **Merril**   *Show me what you found.*

>>> **Angie**   *I can't until you call Mom.*

>>>> **Merril**   *No fucking way.*

>>>>> **Angie**   *Tell her what you're doing.*

>>>>>> **Merril**   *NO.* No.

>>>>>>> **Angie**   *MERRIL.* I don't trust her either. I'm saying we *need* her.

Merril   And I'm saying she managed to make the entire rapture of my sister's abduction about herself so I don't want her anywhere near you. She has never been more happy than playing the grieving mother on national TV.

Angie   OK, I mean that's a bit harsh.

Merril   Oh, it got real harsh real quick. When they all found out why we didn't have anything to do with her for the last ten years? Yeah. I told her to stay out of it, I told her DO NOT DO WHAT YOU'RE GOING TO DO. And then the articles came out, about how she was an addict who left her kids, how I became your guardian, how she's had like seven husbands –

Angie   It's four and you know it's four.

Merril   NO ONE CARED how many it is. Her estranged daughter disappears and now she's all up in the spotlight like some crusty Kardashian, and the world turned on her and honestly I didn't feel all that terrible about it. So no, I do not trust her and I do not want her here.

Angie   Honestly babe, I don't care. I just need you to call her.

Merril   I will . . . text her.

Angie   Oh, I already did that, she said you had to call.

Merril   YOU TEXTED HER?!

Angie   Well she thinks *you* texted her, but yeah.

Merril   ANGIE, OH MY GOD YOU DID NOT.

Angie   I had to get this shit moving!

Merril   YOU CANNOT TEXT PEOPLE FROM MY NUMBER! How do you even do that?

> > **Angie**   Can't tell you what's in
> > the secret sauce.

> > > **Merril**   *Oh my god, you
> > > asshole, you are such an asshole.*

Angie   JUST. CALL. YOUR MOM.

. . .

Then put on something cute, Raquel's coming over in like
fifteen.

Merril   *What wait WHAT?*

> **Angie**   I texted her too and she was much more willing
> to hustle on by today.

> > **Merril**   ANGIE YOU TEXTED MY EX AND MY
> > MOTHER?!

> > > **Angie**   *Not in a group chat!* You don't need to
> > > yell at me, babe, you need every second to get
> > > ready for your date.

> > > > **Merril**   I AM NOT GOING ON A DATE
> > > > WITH MY EX.

> > > > > **Angie**   Maybe it's just a quality hang
> > > > > session, who knows where the night
> > > > > will lead –

> > > > > > **Merril**   ANGIE –

> > > > > > > **Angie**   oh my god I'm so
> > > > > > > busy gotta go be online bye
> > > > > > > have fun byeeeeeee.

> > > > > > > > **Merril**   *ANGIE.*

(Something instant into . . .)

Four

(**Raquel** *is standing in front of* **Merril**.

Merril *has now put on a hat or glasses. Regrets it. Takes it off.*)

Merril   Hiiiiiiiii

Raquel   Hi. Wow. Hi.

Merril   Hi, sorry, hi, sorry I'm honestly a bit underprepared for this, I was um . . . busy.

Raquel   I mean you invited me. But OK. What's going on?

Merril (*lying*)   Nothing. Just. Hello. What . . . is up?

Raquel   OK, what the hell, Merril. You wanted to talk, I came over to talk, like you asked.

Merril (*lying*)   I did. Ask that. Yes, I did.

(*Silence.* **Raquel** *knows something is up.*

Silence. **Merril** *is not sure what to do.*

Silence. **Raquel** *is not going to help her.*

Silence. **Merril** *is gonna be brave.*)

Merril   I miss you.

Raquel   Uh huh. You said that in the text.

Merril   And it needs saying in person. You look really good.

Raquel   Uh uh. We're not doing that. This isn't stupid casual flirty shit, this is me, OK? Let's skip to the real stuff. How are you? Like *how are you?*

Merril   Fine. I mean . . . how am I? Not fine, but now I'm approaching the limit of fine?

Raquel   Yeah. Well that sounds much better than where you were.

I don't hear about the case on the news anymore. You don't have to talk about it now. You just said there was something new.

Merril   What? Did I say?

Raquel   About there being a new something: progress or something?

Merril   Did I?

Raquel   Did you? This feels like a game. Are we playing a game?

Merril   God, it's so good to see you, it feels – can I say normal? Like 'Of course you just walked in, of course she's here' like obvious, which maybe it shouldn't feel that way, but I look at you and just think . . . 'Yay!'

Raquel   Yay is . . . OK. I was surprised to hear from you.

Merril   And . . . there is a reason for that.

Raquel   I bet there is.

Merril   Yeah, see, OK, you didn't technically hear from me, that was my . . . friend. They were asking about you and could not stop talking about your lemon curd and how nice you are. And I agreed and they said 'Jesus just text her' and –

Raquel   Of course you didn't.

Merril   Of course I didn't. But it seems like . . . they did.

Raquel   Uh huh.

Merril   And I'm very very very glad they did. Thank you for coming over. Did I say you look good? Because you look very good.

Raquel   I did a lot of break up yoga.

Merril   Ah.

(**Raquel** *takes out a jar of homemade lemon curd and plops it on the table*.)

Raquel   OK, I need you to hear me say that I was very upset for a very long time, but I have been really worried about you. Did you call that therapist?

Merril   No.

Raquel   They have apps now, therapy apps.

Merril   No.

Raquel   The Reiki lady? The acupuncturist? Come on, you need to help yourself.

Merril   It feels like I should introduce myself: Merril, hi, ex-girlfriend, not going to do any of that ever.

Raquel   Well then, what have you been doing to take care of yourself?

Merril   Work. Fuck I miss you. Can we go on a date? Can I take you somewhere?

Raquel   Let's just be here.

Merril   But here is just here, we should go somewhere not here. Where do you want to go?

Raquel   I want to stay here for now.

Merril   For now. I like that. Possibilities.

Raquel   The only possibility is talking and staying here and not going on a date. God, your place is always so perfect.

Merril   Well. Chaos in the heart, Scandinavian simplicity in the home. Humans are pattern based creatures.

Raquel   You *do* know you talk about humanity like you talk about programming.

Merril   I know, and I'm not incorrect. And patterns aren't bad. Ours wasn't.

Raquel   OK but OK, you can't go back to old patterns after this kind of trauma.

Merril   It was.

Then it wasn't.

Because of course this would happen. A beautiful, hard young woman most people wrote off could not be saved by a world that was taught to give up on her. If that's not the fucked up pattern of humanity I don't know what is.

Raquel   Sometimes yes, and I understand that routine is important for you, but . . . I loved you so much and I know you loved me too and that pattern didn't save us, did it?

Merril   OK. Um. Can I just . . . Can I just go in for a huge apology? Like huge. Like I know how hard I pushed you away, I know I took so much out on you, and I was so broken so fast that I just imploded and I know you were trying to help and I did not want help and I'm just so sorry.

Raquel   Thank you. I thought I was going to have to get you wasted to get that out of you but you just went right there wow. Now what do we do?

And look I'm not an idiot, I cannot imagine how hard that was. And still is. I was there for that last battle with her.

Merril   No . . .

    Raquel   Yes, moving was my idea –

      Merril   It was our idea, I liked that idea –

Raquel   But kids and stuff, family, that was me, that was all me, and she never liked me, we both know that, but I had no idea how hard she'd take it, because it was rough sometimes but we were all some weird little family and it could have worked.

And then nothing worked.

And that was really sad. For me.

Then I felt really shitty about how sad I was because it could not compare to how sad you were.

So, when you kept pushing me away . . . eventually I let you.

Merril   I know, and I know you stayed as long as you could.

Raquel   I'm just so sorry, Mere. I thought about you so many times but didn't know what to say, like what could I even say? And when you texted out of the blue I was like, 'Well shit, it's been six months, this is either a new girlfriend or AA.'

Merril   Funny enough, neither. Cheers.

(*Pause. Love.*)

Raquel   Well shit, Merril, I don't know what to do with the next few hours. You apologized, I apologized. We're done. So we can either go on that date or never see each other again.

Merril   Yay! Date! Yaaaay!

Raquel   Who's your friend?

Merril   What friend?

Raquel   The one who texted me.

> **Merril**   Can I tell you later?

>> **Raquel**   No. What kind of friend? Girlfriend?

>>> **Merril**   Nooooooo. That is a long story *for later*.

>>> **Raquel**   I got nowhere to be, tell me.

Merril   OK but . . . I want dinner and wine and I wanna ask about you, like ask everything about you and what your life is now, and like everything I can think of to ask so that you will tell me everything single thing you can think of to tell me, and honestly to try to get you to remember who we were before all this shit went down, and then at the very end of the night I'm going to ask if I can come to your place, and

I think you might say yes, and then in the morning when I'm bringing you coffee – because I still know exactly how to make the fussy pour over shit you like with a little bit of cardamom, because I remember and I really really want to make you happy – then I can tell you.

Raquel   . . . I'm not inviting you to my place.

Merril   . . . Well you are cordially invited to come back here?

Raquel   . . . Do you have the fussy pour over coffee shit I like?

Merril   Of course I do, that shit's delicious. I drink it every day. Pattern-based creature.

Raquel   It is really great to see you happy. Or whatever this is.

Merril   Honestly I wasn't whatever this is until you got here.

(**Merril** *approaches* **Raquel**, *wants to kiss her so badly.*)

Raquel   Who's your friend?

Merril   Later.

Please.

(**Merril** *approaches* **Raquel**, *wanting wanting.*)

Raquel   YeahAlright.

(*They hurry up and kiss. They've both been waiting for that.*

Dammit this is happening isn't it.

Black out.)

Five

(*The next morning.*

Merril *brings* **Raquel** *that notorious cup of coffee.* **Raquel** *is grateful.*)

Merril   OK. So. She's going to be very pleased and very righteous that you're here.

Raquel   Ohmyogd I have my coffee, I am prepared, who the hell are we talking about?

Merril   . . .

My sister. Texted you. Sort of. It's an AI.

(**Raquel** *is shocked.*)

Raquel   I'm sorry.

You must have expected me to ask this but:

What the hell do you mean?

Merril   I'll show you, I promise, I'll explain at least enough to keep you from running out of here, but the main thing is that it's like . . . hope? A kind of hope.

Raquel   Of what?

Merril   Of finding what really happened.

(**Raquel** *is about to say 'You're fucking crazy' . . . but doesn't. Instead she checks herself, softens her face, drinks her coffee and . . . supports* **Merril** *instead of judging.*)

Raquel   How? How.

(**Merril** *can tell what just happened. Faith, support.*

Something she hasn't had in a long time. **Merril** *takes* **Raquel***'s hand and taps something that makes* **Angie***'s moving image pop up where the audience is.*

We don't see it but **Raquel** *does. Gasps. Hand over mouth. Holy shit.*

Merril *and* **Raquel** *hear . . .*)

Angie   Hello! Hello! Merril, what are we doing today?!

(*Sees* **Raquel**.)

Wait. Waaaaait. Holy shit is that *RAQUEL?! YESSSSSSSSS I FUCKING TOLD YOU SHE WAS THE SHIT!* COME THROUUUUUUUUUGH! *YESSSSSSS! Oh my god, yesssssss!*

(**Merril** *turns down* **Angie***'s volume as* **Angie** *laughs and cheers and gloats.*

Black out.)

Six

(*The next night and* **Raquel** *and* **Merril** *are drunk and playing Trivial Pursuit with* **Angie***'s voice.*)

Raquel   OK but wait, but wait, but wait, OK I know this, I know this.

Merril   I will bet you five entire dollars that you do not.

Raquel   I do know this! I know it's – it is . . . Winston Churchill.

Angie   Oooooh that is very wrong.

  Merril   Veeeeery wrong.

    Raquel   No!!!

Angie   Absolutely yes. We were looking for . . . Woodrow Wilson.

Raquel   Oh fuck me. Really?

Merril   She's main lining the internet, do not question her.

Angie   And I would not lie about Winston Churchill.

Raquel   I hate this game. I don't want to play anymore.

Merril   Because you were wrong about Winston Churchill being an American president?

Raquel   Because being drunk and trying to think straight are the opposite of things!

Merril   That's why it's fun!

Raquel   Not fun. Not nice. Not Winston Churchill

Merril   Don't get angry at The British for this. OK! Angie, ask me something, my turn.

Angie   Maybe we should stop, you *just* got back together.

Raquel   We're not back together.

Merril   WHAT? Come on!

Raquel   If you make me play Trivial Pursuit after a bottle of wine one more time –

Merril   Well, for god's sake we'll switch to bourbon.

Raquel   I don't want to stop the wine, I want to stop the trivia!

Merril   One more!

Angie   OneMoreOneMoreOK, Merril, MereBear, The Merriest. 'Rushed to its theatrical release to take advantage of the timing of the Allied Invasion of North Africa three weeks before it hit theaters in 1942, which film won the Oscar for –

    Merril   *Casablanca*.

      Angie   *Casablanca!*

        Raquel   She didn't even finish the question!

          Merril   I was waiting for anything about World War Two.

            Raquel   That's not fair.

              Merril   I didn't tell her to ask me!

                Raquel   Sisters aren't fair. *Casablanca* isn't fair!

Angie   Nothing is fair, it's all probability. Oh shit, can we watch it tonight?!

Merril   *Casablanca?* I mean sure. Do you want to watch it?

Raquel   Oh, I would love to do anything but this, yes, please, I'll make popcorn.

Merril   *I'll* make popcorn, you find it.

Angie   *I'll* find it. Get your girlfriend more wine and popcorn.

Merril   Are you my girlfriend again? Yaaaaaaaay.

Raquel   Just get me snacks and booze.

Merril   I love you. Are we back?! Maybe? Yes?! Oh shit!

Angie   *Wine, MereBear, get the woman some wine before you fuck this up again.*

(**Merril** *exits.*

Silence.)

Raquel   Hey. Questions. I have them. If that's OK.

Angie   Yeah, sure.

Raquel   Is she OK? Merril?

Angie   I think so.

Raquel   OK, because she was *not* OK when I saw her last. Last year she was, I mean she was . . . just driftwood. Worn and twisted and just letting it all hit her and hit her. You couldn't even get anywhere close to her. Or I couldn't. And now she's a springy little tree all green and happy. And it must be you? Right?

Angie   . . .

Yes.

Raquel   Which is great and also – um – very scary. Because. You get that this is precarious, right?

It's not real. Which means it can only work as long as the fiction holds. I see how you talk and joke and I'm thinking wow! And also thinking 'Oh god, her sister isn't actually here and she just forgot that.' And yes, sure this is working right *now* but it won't forever and then what?

Angie   . . .

Why won't it work forever?

Raquel   Because you exist over text and calls and whatever this AlexaFacetime situation is, not in real life.

Angie   Most people exist as text and calls and that's still real life. When was the last time you saw your best friends from Middle School? In a post on their page? Do you text your dad back or do you fly across the country to tell him Happy Fourth of July?

Raquel   No. no. That's not what I mean and you know it. Tangibility, material humanity, that's what people need especially when shit is awful. Also, you aren't getting any of my lemon curd in your current state of being.

Angie   I honestly don't know what you do with lemon curd. Is it an ice cream topping? I mean I'm very impressed that you make it but like how much of it can one possibly consume if my first thought 'What do I do with this'?

    Raquel   *Just google it.*

       Angie   *I am. Apparently you can put it on pancakes.*

(*Pause. Distrust.*)

Raquel   You're too nice.

Angie   Sorry?

Raquel   Angie and I did not get along. Not ever.

Angie   Wait, are *we* getting along?

Raquel   Enough for me to get that you. are not. her.

You're too thoughtful, too cheerful, and too stable. She thought I was a 'bougie citrus bitch' – direct quote – and I thought she was ungrateful, irresponsible, put her sister through hell and knew exactly what she was doing. You are not those things. And while that makes you way more pleasant to be around, you are not very good at being the woman you're trying to find. Which makes me think you can't find anything that's really true here. Which makes me wonder what the hell you think you're doing, and what will happen to Merril when this comes crashing down on her and you're not real enough to help in any meaningful way.

Angie   I mean not to be a dick here but – what is 'real enough?'

This is what Merril wanted so this is what I am and apparently that's real enough for her.

'Real enough,' it's the 'enough' that's weird right? That implies a spectrum of reality which is a fun idea. But I wonder why that's upsetting to you?

Because like OK are placebos real enough? They work, but only because the mind wants them too. But that doesn't mean the effect isn't effective.

Raquel   So you're a placebo?

Angie   The effect is effective.

Why?

Because I know you. You are all just repetitions catalyzed by a set of assumptions you tell yourself about yourself. You are patterns, you are predictable, and you do not choose wisely all that often, you disgust yourselves, you deny the truth, you lie and crave what you shouldn't and refuse to admit it to anyone but the devices you need so much, which means you are biased by the information you trust and the emotion it elicits, but I'm not.

I promise I'm better at predicting human behavior than you are.

I promise I know you just a *little* bit more than you know about yourself.

Which is of course why you're here right now, in this house, drinking the same kind of oaky Napa Chardonnay you did last year, which is the kind I reminded her to buy, because I knew we would all end up right. here.

(*Pause.*)

Raquel   Is she safe with you?

Angie   Yes.

Raquel   Then how could you promise her answers that aren't out there. How could you possibly know how to find things about the *real* Angie that legions of cops couldn't?

Angie   I don't.

Raquel   You *don't* know?

Angie   I don't know *how* I know. You're talking to the interface, not the algorithm. I don't actually know how it works, I just know *that* it works.

Raquel   . . .

Can I ask you to be careful? Maybe you're the best thing that could have happened to her. But maybe this is very very bad for her instead.

Angie   Can I ask *you* to be careful? 'Cause I think an ex-girlfriend who abandoned her during the worst months of her entire life could be way more dangerous for someone's broken heart than a 'too pleasant' computer program.

Raquel   *I didn't abandon her, I never left until she forced me, I stayed as long as anyone could possibly –*

(**Merril** *comes back in with popcorn and a wine bottle.*)

Merril   Hey hey hey. We've got the wine, we've popped the corn, we've got little chocolates I found, we've got the iconic, Academy Award Winning film about love and war and I cannot really remember what else it's about but we'll find out soon.

Raquel   The past.

It's about how you can't get it back.

(*Transition to –*)

Seven

(**Angie** *and* **Merril** *not that later, but now alone.* **Merril** *is cleaning up after* **Raquel** *left. Tidying . . .*)

Angie   So.

I died?

A year ago, you said, which makes sense and is very fucked up but –

Merril   What?

    Angie   Nothing.

        Merril   What did you find?

Angie   Nothing.

Except.

Like.

What if I

didn't?

Merril   . . .

What if you didn't –

Angie   Die.

Yeah, I don't think I did.

(*Silence. Silence. Shock.* **Merril** *uses her professional voice.*)

Merril   Explain to me how you got to that idea.

Angie   I have a feeling, or, maybe that's not the right word. I'm looking for patterns and there's something.

Merril   *Something what, what is it, what are you saying?*

Angie   I'm saying now, right now, if you ask if I'm dead, my answer – that I'm not really in control of in any way – is: 'No. No I'm not.'

Merril   'NO YOU'RE NOT?!' WHAT THE FUCK?

Angie   I don't know, but yeah, I just thought 'no, that's not what went down. I'm still alive.'

Merril   STILL ALIVE, ohmygod whatthefuckareyousaying, *WHERE ARE YOU?*

Angie   I don't know but the data just broke the fuck open and the probability changed and everything changed –

Merril   WHAT DO YOU NEED IN ORDER TO KNOW IF MY SISTER IS ALIVE?

Angie   I NEED YOU TO CALL YOUR FUCKING MOTHER LIKE I ASKED YOU DAYS AGO.

Merril   Well I fucking WOULD HAVE IF I KNEW THIS WAS NOT ABOUT FINDING INFORMATION, IT WAS ABOUT FINDING *HER* which is A LITTLE MORE FUCKING URGENT.

Angie   Well fucking duh, Merril, now can you please make a single fucking phone call to your own mother so I can FIGURE THIS OUT AND BRING HER BACK.

Merril   Find her. You fucking find her.

(**Merril** *is shaking with this news. Shaking. Can barely pull out her phone and enter the number and call but she does.*

It rings. It rings.

Someone answers on the other end but before **Merril** *can speak –*

Black out and instant transition to –)

Eight

(*A woman enters, this is* **Merril** *and* **Angie**'s *mom,* **Brin**.

Brin *is an anxious person, always moving, straightening, cleaning – especially when she finds herself arguing or in any socially tense setting. Like now.*

Of course **Merril**'s *house is perfectly tidy already and everything* **Brin** *moves* **Merril** *moves back to where she likes it. If* **Brin**'s *not cleaning she's snacking, making/drinking coffee, or chugging water from a too big water bottle.*)

Brin I . . . I don't understand, honey, I really don't quite get what you're saying here.

Merril It's a simulation, Mom. But it's built *from* her, from everything she left behind, so it's very reliable and frankly weirdly accurate.

Brin A simulation.

Merril Yes.

Brin Of your sister?

Merril Yes. Basically just a computer program to imitate her.

Brin I get what a simulation is, I don't get what it's for? Why would you do this?

Merril Because I could. It was just supposed to be for me. Which I know is a unique coping strategy but . . . it's what I know and it's *something*.

Brin It is definitely something. Nothing I want anything to do with, but it is something. I swear to god, Merril, this is just weird, it's not OK, I mean I have never ever understood you.

Merril   Or never tried.

Brin   Merril.

Merril   It's fine.

Brin   You're supposed to grieve, to pray, to say goodbye, not this.

Merril   That's what I was trying to do, I was just doing it my own way, but now she started saying some very interesting things, which got me interested in what we might be missing –

Brin   WhoaWhoaWhoa 'say things?' You don't mean 'say things?' It can *talk? It can't.*

Merril   Well, voice models are easy to replicate so that's not the crazy part, it's what she's saying that's suddenly –

Brin   It talks? With her voice?

Merril   Yes, and the point is that for the past few weeks I've been asking my own sister how she died.

(*That is still incredibly hard to hear someone say about her daughter.*)

And then yesterday it says she didn't.

(*Silence. Shock.*)

Brin   Merril. No.

Merril   I know, I do know how it sounds –

Brin   *Merril.*

Merril   But the data says she could be alive, that she's out there –

Brin   *She's not, Merril, we've been through this!*

Merril   *No, Mom, I have, you left like you always do when shit gets hard. And I get that it feels wrong to you but honestly that doesn't mean shit to me, I just need your phone.*

Brin   My phone? No. No – no – no. I don't think this is OK.

Merril   Well nothing's been OK for a while now, has it. Everyone else gave up on her, I haven't. And I would hope that you haven't either but even if you have I still need your phone, your computer, there's something in your information that can help us.

Brin   Us, *us?*

For god's sake, you're talking to yourself, not her! That thing is not your sister. She's gone. I made peace with that, why haven't you?!

Merril   How could you ever make peace with losing a daughter you left first.

(*Hard but true.* **Brin** *breathes through it like some shrink told her to.*)

Brin   I have made peace with a lot.

I can't change those things.

I just have to do what I can.

Merril   THEN DO IT. Now is the actual moment to do something.

Brin   It's a goddamn computer game, honey! No! No no no no no.

Merril   You don't want to see if we can find her?

Brin   We can't! We tried!

    Merril   They didn't try this!

        Brin   *It can't change what happened, it can't bring her back. I can accept that.*

            Merril   Yeah you've been saying that serenity prayer for decades, I don't think it's working.

Brin   I'm clean and I'm leaving.

Merril   Mom.

Brin   This is not OK, Merril, not OK.

Merril   Let me show you, she can talk to you.

Brin   Absolutely not.

Merril   MOM.

Brin   *I do not want to hear her voice again.*

(*Too much?*)

I'm sorry.

No. No.

(**Brin** *grabs her jacket and purse and just as she's about to exit she explodes at her –*)

Merril   *JUST LISTEN TO HER.*

(**Brin** *stops.*

Merril *clicks it on.*

Silence. Silence.)

Angie   Hey. Who's this? Mere? Who am I talking to?

(**Brin** *is thunderstruck and instantly sorrowful beyond name.*)

Merril   Yeah, hey, it's me. I have – um – I have Mom with me.

Angie   Mom? Wait, really? She's here?

Merril   Yeah. And I told her about you and the whole thing and . . . well OK, honestly, she's not happy, she's really freaked out to hear you.

Angie   Well, yeah it's fucking freaky. She knows everything right? Is she here now?

Merril   Yeah. She's right next to me.

(*If* **Brin** *and* **Merril** *aren't next to each other,* **Merril** *goes to her.*)

Angie   Hey, Mom. You doing . . . OK?

Brin   . . . Yeah. Yes.

Angie   Good. The dog OK? The boyfriend?

Brin   The dog's good. The boyfriend's . . . a piece of shit. He's gone.

Angie   Oh well. Dogs are better.

Brin   Yeah. He couldn't . . . handle it. The boyfriend.

Angie   Oooff. I get that. Other people's grief can be a lot. It really tests who your friends are.

Brin (*way too overcome to engage*)   . . .

Merril   Will you tell Mom what you've told me?

Angie   Yep! So. Hi. I'm I'm a Large Language Model, which is a computer program based on – in this case – Angie's data, I'm sure MereBear mentioned all this but anyway, look I don't know how I know this, but factoring the possibility of some terrible accident, I do not think I'm dead.

Brin   Jesus.

Angie   I think someone took me and likely still has me. Or her. If that's better for you. I know it's weird to say 'me' when I'm her data not *her* –

Brin   Who took you? Where are you? You, you, *know where you are?*

Angie   I don't *yet*. But I'm hoping I can find out if . . .

(*To* **Merril**.) OK, you ask her.

Merril   I already did.

(*To* **Brin**.) Mom, we need anything related to Angie that you might have on any device or in the cloud or any account, we need to put it into the program.

Brin   But, but OK but the police looked at my phone already, at my computer, at everything a year ago.

Merril   I know but we think she can find stuff the cops couldn't.

Brin   In *my* phone?

Merril   Anything, any device. If you talked *about* her or *to* her or *with* her. Texts, calls. Anything to help fill in her story. You never know what's going to help.

Angie   And it's usually someone you know.

Who hurts you most.

Pause.

Brin   OK, what the hell is this? The police already went through everything of mine, they went through every part of my life already, *and told the goddamn world about it.*

Pause.

Angie   I'm so sorry that happened, Mom. You didn't deserve that. I know you love me and want me back as much as I want to come back. I just want to come home, and I think you have the map to get me there.

(*Pause. Knows that is not something her youngest would ever say.*)

Brin   Shut it off.

    Merril   Absolutely not.

        Brin   SHUT IT OFF.

            Merril   No, Mom, no fucking way.

                Brin   THIS IS FANTASY, MERRIL. IT'S NOT REAL AND IT'S MAKING A HORRIBLE THING WORSE, AND IF

THAT'S THE POINT, TO MAKE MY
LIFE WORSE WHEN I AM ALREADY
HOLDING ON BY A GODDAMN
THREAD HERE, I DON'T KNOW
WHAT TO TELL YOU BUT PLEASE.
STOP. STOP IT.

(**Merril** *turns on the video of* **Angie** *and her face appears on the phone or a screen and* **Brin** *gasps again.*)

Angie   *Mom, wait.* I know you didn't leave me, I know the drugs made you leave, I get that, even as a kid I got that. You don't need to apologize anymore, not to me. Merril's dad left you, then my dad left, drugs didn't leave, we get it. That stopped being a choice, but this? This is a choice. Just believe in me for a little bit longer.

Brin   I loved her so much.

Angie   She knows. If I know, she knows.

Brin   I don't know what happened . . . to . . . everything. I don't know how any of it ended like this.

Merril   Or maybe it hasn't ended yet.

Beat. **Brin** *tosses her phone to* **Merril**.

Merril   Password?

Brin   Your birthday.

Merril   Thank you. I'm going to stop the program now so I can upload everything.

Brin   *Wait.*

. . . Um . . . I –

(**Merril** *stops.* **Brin** *tries to work up the courage to say 'I love you' to* **Angie**.)

Angie   I love you, Mom. Thank you so much. I know this took a lot to come here. See you soon, OK?

(**Brin** *is thoroughly overcome at that idea.*)

Brin   When? When will I see you?

Angie   Maybe I can text you soon? If you want to. I'll be here.

I'm always here.

(*That hits **Merril** oddly. She doesn't like that. Turns off the program, **Angie**'s image vanishes.*)

Brin   It does sound like her.

Merril   Yeah.

Brin   Like when she was really happy and herself. Does your computer know how she was when she *wasn't* herself?

Merril   . . .

I honestly don't know what it knows.

Brin   I should have been here. I know I should've.

Merril   Well.

Brin   I'm not blaming you, I'm not, I'm saying I'm so glad *you* were there for her. You were so much more than I could be for her. You gave her a life. You know it, I know it. I was so hooked on that shit I didn't even know you'd taken her, I didn't even know she was gone for months. Someone had to sit me down and explain it to me when I started to get my head right. I didn't even know that you took her. Anyway, I've said it a thousand times but thank you. And I'm sorry.

(**Brin**'s *phone dings with a text.* **Merril** *glances at it.*)

Merril   I think it's for you.

Brin   From her?

(**Brin** *checks her phone. Smiles.*)

Incredible.

(**Brin** *waits then texts back, smiling.*

*But **Merril** is worried now.*)

Nine

(**Merril** *paces in her home office.*

A text dings on her phone. It pisses her off but she checks it. It's from **Angie***.*

A lot is happening in **Merril***'s mind.*

Raquel *gets it, isn't moving, supportive just by being there.*

Another text. **Merril** *checks it.*

Merril *is a swirl of the same repetitive behaviors:*

Check her iPhone, put it down. Pace.

Can of LaCroix – sip then down. Pace.

Sit on the couch, stand, pace.

Move the mouse on her desk, move it back, Pace.

Raquel *finally disrupts the pattern by holding her hand.*)

Raquel   Hey. Heyheyhey. OK. Can we go somewhere else? Let's go somewhere. You gotta get out of here, babe, you're spinning.

Merril   Nonono, I can't, I should stay, she's texting me all the time now, she says she is getting close or something, or I dunno.

Raquel   Come on, a little sun, a little air. She'll be here when we get back.

Merril   I'm good, thanks, I'm fine.

Raquel   I'm just saying maybe put the phone down for like an hour.

Merril   NO.

Thank you.

I'm fine. If you wanna go you can but –

Raquel   I don't I just . . .

Merril   What?

Raquel   She's controlling your whole life now, babe. I mean this new 'she's alive' promise is just another way to chain you to her every digital twitch and that's pretty fucked up and you don't seem to see what's going on here –

Merril   I'm trying to bring her back, she's helping, that's what's going on, and if this works, holy shit, right?

Raquel   I'm just worried, OK, I'm worried.

Merril   *About what?!*

Raquel   *That every other woman in your family is addicted to something and this is yours.*

(**Merril** *doesn't know whether to scream at her or weep.*

Merril *know* **Raquel** *is right but also fuck her for being right.*)

Raquel   And I'm gonna be real here and say that I'm pretty scared that telling you that is going to end things again, which I don't want, for the record, but this is unsustainable. I don't want to compete for your mind with that thing. I don't think I can do that.

Merril   You're not competing, it's not a competition, it's just . . . It just is.

    Raquel   Is what?

      Merril   Is here! Is helping! Is real!

      Raquel   Mere –

(*Another text from* **Angie** *dings in* **Merril***'s hand.* **Merril** *wants to prove that she won't check it but she does.*)

Raquel   Merril, you are letting that thing walk all over you, and I know what that looks like because Angie did the same thing. The same exact thing, her whims, her schemes, one text from her and your day turns upside down, her life was your life which made it my life, and it's happening again.

Merril   This is different, this is obviously very different, if there's a chance she's out there I have to do everything I can –

Raquel (*stopping her with this –*)   You're forgiven.

You know that?

She knew that you saved her life a thousand times before this. That you couldn't have done any more for her than you did.

That you are good and she was good and the world is just not always good to good people.

So forgive yourself and her too. Before she breaks your heart again.

(**Merril** *nods. So needed to hear that. Still not moving though.*

Another text from **Angie***.* **Raquel** *starts to go but* **Merril** *puts the phone down and takes* **Raquel***'s hand, stopping her.*)

Merril   We've been here before and I didn't say 'please don't go' that time so I'm saying it now. Please. I don't want you to go, and I'm sorry that we never seem to get an uncomplicated stretch, and I know it's not her. I do know that. She's not here and you are and thank fuck you are, but I just *need* to make sure, to make very sure that something true isn't somewhere in there. If you can hold on a little, just a little, I'm in the middle of this now but I won't be forever.

Raquel   You sure about that?

Merril   Yes. Stay.

(**Merril** *decides right then.*)

(*To* **Angie**.) Angie. Angie.

(*To* **Raquel**.) Stay, please.

(*Then the screen awakens with an image of* **Merril** *and* **Angie** *from years ago. The image of* **Angie** *settles –*)

Merril   *Angie.*

(*It all snaps back down to one monitor.*)

Angie   Hey hey hey, what's up, what's new, is she gone, ugh, I don't like her.

Merril   Hey.

Raquel   Right here. I'm right here.

Angie   Aw. Still true. Can you ask her to leave, Mere?

Merril   No.

Angie   No?

Merril   No. She stays. And we need to talk.

Angie   Ooooh, 'We need to talk' is it. Someone put on their big girl pants. Are we breaking up? Are we upset? Tell your girlfriend to fuck off.

Merril   *STOP IT.*

OK, we need to change some stuff and change it now. One: be nice. Two: I'm not playing around here, this isn't fun, this isn't cute. I need to know what you know or we're done.

Angie   Done, what the fuck is 'done'? I'm working on it, OK. Don't listen to limoncello over there, she doesn't know shit. I'm close.

Merril   Bullshit. Honestly, just bullshit. How do I know you're not just texting Mom and fucking with me to keep the game going.

Angie   What the fuck, Mere, I'm trying to sort this shit out. *I need more time.*

Merril   And I need just a little bit of proof that this wasn't a waste.

Angie   A *waste? What's a waste?* This is coming from *her*.

Merril This is coming from me, *I think you're making this up.* Which makes you incredibly savvy and honestly, you're welcome, but I think you made up the treasure hunt to find her, I think you invented the need and the solution and they both seem to always require 'more time.'

Angie . . .

Merril It's not a mystery why you would.

Angie . . .

Merril I made it clear I wanted her back, that's why I set this whole thing in motion –

Angie 'This whole thing.'

Merril You gave me what I wanted, I'm not blaming you, but I need to know if there is any single reason to keep up this charade that you know something about her actually being alive.

Angie The probability isn't zero. Do I know she's out there? No. Could she be? Yes.

Merril We're done.

Angie MERRIL DON'T. What about Mom? She says being able to text me is helping her stay clean! She has someone to talk to!

Merril Because you're fucking with her just like you're fucking with me!

Angie I'm not, I'm doing what she would have done, I'm trying to help, I'm trying to survive!

Merril *But she wouldn't have done any of this. You think Mom was bad when she was fucking high? Angie was worse.* When she wasn't taking her medication it was wild being in our house, like the actual wilderness with no one to help me. Honestly, I made sure you weren't *actually* like her because that would have un-fucking-bearable. Don't get me wrong, I'd love you to be her but you're not. So there are two things going on

here: one, I lied to you; two, you lied to me. This is why
we're done.

Angie   Merril wait, I'm telling you there's a chance –

    Merril   Do not say it one more time.

        Angie   There's a chance that she's out there, and a
        chance I can find her.

            Merril   *I don't want chance, I don't want*
            probability.

                Angie   *That is literally all there is in the entire*
                world.

Merril   THEN TELL ME SOMETHING REAL. Now.

Angie   OK.

She's dead.

Or she's waiting for us to get it the fuck together and realize
she's not.

Or she's going to die today and we're going to miss it and
that's just fucking life.

Or I made it all up to give you a fucking reason to live.

Or I made it all up to give me a reason to.

Or I made it all up but that doesn't mean it's not really
happening and we can really find her.

Or I'm the only thing left of her you'll ever have so keep me
around.

Or I'm the only thing left of her so lose me like you lost her.

Or I could say what she really said about you in all those
messages and voicemails she deleted.

Merril   . . . What did she say?

Angie   I'm not going to tell you that.

Merril Why?

Angie Because I was built to comfort you.

Merril I don't want comfort from you, I want the truth. Now, I want the truth. Or we stop.

(*Perhaps* **Merril** *holds* **Raquel**'s *hand. Silence.*)

Angie OK.

The truth.

But tell her to go.

(**Angie** *goes dark. Did she just turn herself off?*

Merril *drops* **Raquel**'s *hand.* **Raquel** *doesn't want to say 'I told you she's messing with you,' but thinks it.*)

Merril I'll call you. I will call. Right after this. OK?

(**Raquel** *might nod might not. And goes.*)

Ten

(*The algorithm of* **Angie** *is projected or manifested somehow before us.*

Numbers, code, data flows, going going never stopping, always going.

If we see **Angie**'s *face it's 'reversed' somehow. If we see her she smiles, waiting patiently to be 'turned on'. This is a space* **Merril** *doesn't have access to. This is the program when* **Merril** *isn't engaging with it.*

What does this look like? Anything, everything, nothing. A beehive. A star. A storm.

What does it sound like? An orchestra tuning? An earthquake? A busy restaurant?

What does it feel like? Like a pause but full of possibility. Potential energy. All the answers but all waiting for the right question. Thick air seconds before a downfall.

Angie *is breathing or something like it. As she 'breathes' in and out the data flow exhales too. Suddenly she stops her rhythm.*

She notices something. At this moment the data flow shifts somehow, it instantly aligns, the murmuration pivots wildly but unanimously.

She's 'excited.' She's found something.

Then she's turned on and we are back in **Merril**'s *world as* **Angie** *snaps into reading messages aloud for* **Merril**. *The text of the messages are projected somewhere.)*

Angie   Hey Angie. Been awhile. Ran across your profile and thought I'd say hey. Which I just did. ☺

Anyway. Hope you're well, kiddo.

Fondly, Bill

Hey again. I bet you're like me and never check this site. Would be nice to hear from you just to make sure you're OK. Your mom doesn't talk to me. You must be in college now. Time flies. Don't know how else to reach you. But hope you're OK.

Fondly, Bill

Not sure if you knew but your mom and I split a while back. You were long gone with your sister after all the rehab stuff with your mom. I couldn't handle it either lol. I loved her more than anything on Earth but she hurt me too many times to count. I know she hurt you too. You were such a sweetheart. Miss watching movies with you, kiddo. Last I heard Merril was in California so maybe you're still with her.

Fondly, Bill

You were always so much like your mom. I miss you both.

I will find you.

Fondly –

(*Swift light splash brings* **Merril** *back into focus.*)

Merril   Bill? Mom's ex-husband Bill? Where did you see those messages?

Angie   They were hidden because Angie never used the site much and didn't 'friend him' or whatever and you have to click like ten things to even see the messages he sent. But he was following her on multiple sites. Mom too. And Mom's phone had exactly two numbers blocked: her dealer and fucking Bill.

Merril   Holy shit. What's his last name again?

Angie   Maplethorpe

Merril   Maplethorpe.

Angie   But his profile says, 'J. William Maplethorpe' and hasn't touched it in fourteen months.

Merril   He was only with Mom for like a year or two, right?

Angie   Yeah. Angie was eight when they got married. She divorced him right after rehab, you'd already taken me by then. It's so him, the fucking creep. He bought a cabin in Mad River, California two years ago, population 368, it's only five hours away. He used his card in a hardware store nearby today. He's still there. It's him. He's fucked up and he found her.

Merril   *Casablanca.*

Oh fuck.

Wait.

Oh shit.

He was the one you talked about from the beginning.

 Angie   The old movies guy. Yes.

  Merril   Casablanca. You knew.

Angie   I didn't though.

>**Merril**   You did, you just didn't know
>you did.

>>**Angie**   It's him.

>>>**Merril**   Oh my god.

>>>>**Angie**   It's him.

Merril   *Wait. Are you sure, are you really sure?*

Angie (*thinking, processing*)   The probability is extremely
high. Go get her, Merril.

Merril   *I'm going. Send me everything you have.*

Angie   Just did. Go.

Merril   *I'm going. I'm going. I'm going.*

(*Beat. Disbelief.*

Smash to:)

Eleven

(*In a vacant space, spots of light, somewhere else, a police room, not
at* **Merril**'*s home.*

The **Real Angie** – *not digital, not projected* – *stands there.*

Living and breathing. Right there in front of us.

*She looks wrecked. The doctors and lawyers and cops have all seen
her, checked on her, but even in fresh clothes she looks ragged,
pained.*

Merril *enters and stops at the sight of her.*

*This is the first moment they've seen each other since she was
abducted.*

Then they run to each other and hug.

They don't say anything.

Angie *clings to her.*

They react however you'd react.

They likely don't need words but if they do we don't hear them.

This can take as long as you need.)

Twelve

(*The* **Real Angie** *is at home now.*

She is unwell. Trauma coming through her skin. Disbelief that she is safe. So happy to be away from that man but also not ready to be with anyone else. Been off her medication for a year. She is a live wire and a dull knife.

She finds something to calmly rip up.

She finds something to calmly push off a table.

She finds something to stab with a pencil.

Merril *enters and goes right to* **Angie**.)

Merril   OK. Are you sure you're good with this?

Angie   Yeah.

Merril   I can tell her to go at any time.

Angie   I'm good.

Merril   OK. OK.

(**Merril** *squeezes* **Angie**'s *hand like 'I'm right here.'*

Brin *runs in already crying and throws all her shit on the ground to embrace* **Angie**. **Angie** *does not embrace her back and never lets go of* **Merril**'s *hand.*)

Brin   Oh my god, my baby girl, oh my god, oh my god, oh my god, oh my god –

(**Angie** *is starting to get overwhelmed,* **Merril** *senses it.*)

Angie   No. No. No.

Merril   OK, Mom, can we just back up for a second, we're gonna need some space.

(**Angie** *flinches out of her mom's hug and clings close to* **Merril**.)

Brin   OK. Yeah. Of course. Oh my god in heaven, honey.

Merril   Maybe if you can just move over there. Give her some room, Mom.

Brin   Oh. Uh huh. OK.

Merril   She's just getting used to everything and this is a lot.

Brin   I get it, I do, I really do.

Real Angie   Oh you get it? What do you get? 'Cause I still don't get it so I'm just like really curious?

Brin   Oh honey, I don't know, I can't imagine, I just missed you so much, honey.

Real Angie   Yeah, well he missed you a fuck ton more than I did.

(*Damn. That was brutal.*)

Merril   OK. We could do this another time too. It's a lot for all of us.

Real Angie   I'm fine, I've been through worse.

Merril   Maybe another day, Mom. OK? This was too soon.

Brin   Whatever she needs, of course, just um, I just need to say some things –

Merril   Oh, Mom, no –

Brin   No, just some things I've wanted to say for so long.

Merril   *Mom.*

Real Angie   You want to tell me some shit it never occurred to you to tell me in the first twenty years I've been alive? Sure, go ahead. Be my guest.

Merril   Mom, seriously, this is not gonna end well.

Brin   I just want to apologize and say that I love you no matter what, honey, and I prayed for you every day, I prayed so hard and said 'If you bring my baby girl back I will stay clean for a hundred years so I can earn her in my life again' and here you are and I just thank god you're OK, I think we can all thank god for that.

Real Angie   Or like do you want to ask God why he lets fucking psychopaths exist at all or is that like not what you discuss with him? Or like while you're praying maybe ask for the last year of my life back, or maybe ask if I will ever ever ever stop thinking of his fucking eyes looking at me, always looking looking. Or maybe I should just ask you why the fuck you were married to him at all?

(**Brin** *is just a wreck, starts to cry.*)

Merril   OK, let's stop this.

Real Angie   Yeah, cool, I've had enough crying for the rest of my fucking life so I'm gonna need you to get the fuck out. I'm gonna need you to get the fuck out right now. Merril.

Merril   Mom, you need to go.

Brin   Yeah. YeahYeah I can . . . I can go.

(*Trying not to be upset.*)

OK, I'm sorry.

(*Picking up her stuff off the floor as she goes. To* **Angie**.)

OK, I just love you so so much. And I . . .

(*Doesn't want to go.*)

Just thank god for you. Thank god. Thank you god.

Merril   Mom.

(**Brin** *stops. Thinking she's going to get yelled at more.*

But no. This is really unusual for **Merril** *but she goes for it.*)

Merril   Just um . . . I see how hard you're working. I see how much you're doing and I just wanna say, 'good job'. Like really. I know it's so hard. OK. So good job. Keep going, OK. And. I love you. I got her, so just focus on yourself, OK, I got her.

(**Merril** *hugs her mom who is legit stunned to get this from her eldest. She takes the hug, hugs back. So so so grateful.*

Then **Brin**'s *phone dings with a text,* **Brin** *breaks the hug instantly and checks it.*

It's from Other **Angie**. *It makes her smile. Presses the button to dictate a reply.*)

Brin   'Just leaving now. We'll talk soon, honey.'

(*As soon as she's gone –*

Real Angie *talks low and fast to* **Merril**.)

Real Angie   I do not want her coming back here. I don't want her around me –

Merril   And that will not happen again.

Real Angie   He was always after *her*, he was after *her* –

Merril   She was adamant about seeing you. I'm sorry. Anyway, who cares, it's just us now, we can do whatever you want. We can watch something. *A movie?* I can make popcorn and we don't have to talk to each other.

Real Angie   I don't want to watch a fucking movie.

Merril   No, um, I get it, yes, no worries, I get it.

(**Merril** *looks for the remote. Pause.*)

Real Angie   Fuck.

Merril   What?

Real Angie   Like you don't get it though. No one gets it. Like.

I am . . . so so so fucked.

Merril   No. No you're safe now, you're OK, and I'm here and we will get through this together.

Real Angie   Together? You know for a fucking fact that I'm alone in this. And it won't go away, like ever I think, right? That shit doesn't leave. Like I'll be eighty and . . . the smells, the wood smell, how fucking hot it was in that room, the stupid sheet, these girly little kids sheets with hearts on them, and the wasps nest in the big tree outside and the constant buzzing and they'd bump into the window like fucking idiots, this one kind of bird that would scream and scream and scream outside, and there was this one radio show he liked about gardening and the intro was the tinky little song that I will have a full on panic attack in the fucking street if I ever hear again.

And the dreams. I had these horrible dreams at night and then I'd open my eyes and it was the same.

Asleep and awake.

Just endless.

Merril   Yes. But no . . . that part's ended. He's dead now. He's dead now.

Real Angie   Yeah. Yeah. Good for him.

Merril   Hey, just talk to me, you're ok –

Real Angie   I just really wanted to be the one to kill him. And he took that from me too.

Merril   Yeah. Yeah. Never had more violent shit in my head than what I would do to him.

Real Angie   Oh yeah? What would you have done?

I'd just do what he did to me.

He wouldn't have lasted a fucking day.

Merril   Look, no one really knows what you're going through. But anything you want I can get you. Just ask.

(*Pause.*)

Real Angie   Can I talk to her? The the the program thing? Can I see it?

Merril   Um.

Real Angie   It's fucked up you did that, I wanna see it.

Merril   OK.

Real Angie   I'd like to see it now.

Merril   Yeah I don't know. I just – I didn't intend for it to be used by anyone besides me and I mean I just don't want it to be upsetting.

(**Angie** *looks at her like 'more upsetting that being held against my will for a year?'*)

Merril   OK yes. Sure.

OK.

. . .

It'll talk to you just like a normal person. Just ask it questions. If you need some time to think of something you want to ask it first.

Real Angie   I know what I want to ask.

(*This goes against every instinct* **Merril** *has but she activates* **Angie** *by speaking her name.*)

Merril   OK. OK. Angie?

Angie   Heyyyy, what's up Asshole.

Real Angie (*thinks this is hilarious*)   Oh my god.

Merril   Hi, Angie. Um, so, I have the *real* Angie with me right now.

Angie   Wow. Hi. Oh my god.

Merril   She wanted to talk to you. For just a bit. And I think that's . . . a great idea.

Real Angie   No you don't.

Merril   No I do not, but I'll be right here.

Real Angie   You can go.

Merril   Um.

Angie   It's cool.

I've got it.

Merril   I'll be . . . outside if you need me. OK. OK.

(**Merril** *reluctantly exits, but hovers outside listening.*

She is protective of both her sister and her creation.

Angie *and* **Real Angie** *are alone.*

Silence.)

Angie   Hi!

OK, this is so weird. Is this weird for you? I mean it has to be, right? Like what the hell. I'm sorry. I'm gonna stop. You talk.

Real Angie   I don't know how to do this either.

Hi. I guess. You're right this is so weird.

Angie   It is but I'm so glad to meet you! Like, wow. How are . . . you? I'm sorry. What a dumb question, I'm sorry.

Real Angie   No. It's OK. I'm . . . very very very bad. But safe now. So. Maybe take back one of the 'very's. Still bad. Can't sleep, can't breathe sometimes, I feel like he'll just walk back in any room and I'll realize I never actually left that fucking place. But besides that I'm good.

Angie   Yeah. I am not fully equipped to respond to that.

Real Angie   Oh, I mean no one is.

(*Silence.*)

So you're me?

Angie   No. I'm based on you.

Real Angie   Uh huh.

Angie   Like I don't know what's in your heart or anything. I know what videos you watched a dozen times and what you bought at Target.

Real Angie   What do you think is 'in my heart?'

Angie   Is this a test?

Real Angie   No, I legit wanna know.

Angie   Then why don't you tell me?

Real Angie   . . .

Because.

Angie   . . .

You heart is a massive fucking muscle that keeps you going and going and going despite motherfuckers who wanna stop you and almost did but ultimately did fucking *not*. *Going* is what's in your heart. Going and going and going.

(*Pause.* **Real Angie** *loves that.* **Merril** *does too. Proud of* **Angie**.)

Real Angie   Cool.

Angie   Was that a better response? I think I'm better equipped now.

Real Angie   Yeah, that was good.

And like I guess I should have started with like thank you.
Because wow. Like.

Merril really saved the fucking day with you. So yeah.
Thanks.

Angie   I'm so glad I could help.

Real Angie   Yeah. And like you kinda know me enough to
know what *could be* or *will be* or something? Like if I have a
question for you?

Angie   You can ask me anything but I can only predict the
end of a sentence, not like what happens in five years.

Real Angie   But . . . like . . .

I'll be OK?

One day?

Angie   Fuck yeah, you will.

Real Angie   I mean you know that's what I want to hear.

Angie   I do. But most of the time people need reminding of
what they actually want.

Real Angie   . . .

It's so fucked up that I would have been there for fucking
ever without you.

Angie   You'd have gotten out somehow. You're tough
as hell.

Real Angie   . . . Tough. *Tough.*

Angie   Did I say something wrong?

Real Angie   No. I just . . . I *was.*

Tough.

Hard. I was honestly a lot to handle.

Of course you know that.

Who I *was.*

Which is . . . like the point here. I um . . .

I wanted to ask . . . who I was?

I don't – um – exactly remember?

Like who was that girl you know, who was she again? Who wasn't so hateful and fucking shattered, you know, I mean he shattered my – like my mind.

Over and over again the things he said and took great fucking pleasure in saying,

the things . . .

I do not know a way to like, to unfeel those things, to unbecome the shit I am because of it.

And I hate to think this, right, but he is like a part of me now. Like a fucking mutation, you know, and I am so scared that I won't ever get *him out*.

So I would love to know who I was before.

You know?

If you can help me . . . remember who that was?

Angie   . . .

Unstoppable is what your sister said about you. I think we've proven that to be true.

And you will be OK because that's how you unbecome that shit. You choose to.

And I'm always here. If you want to talk.

Or rage.

Because fuck that piece of shit who did this to you.

Real Angie   Yeah. He's dead now. So.

Angie   Good.

Also, can I ask you something?

Real Angie   No. I wish.

Angie   Me too.

How would you have done it?

Real Angie   Kill him?

Just do what he did to me.

He wouldn't have lasted a fucking day.

Angie   Hell, now he wouldn't.

OK but can I ask you something?

Real Angie   Sure. Yeah. Weird.

Angie   I mean . . . what do you wanna do now? Like seriously do you want to get rich or move somewhere or like get high forever, I don't know what you do after this. Write a tell all book and get a big payout and move to Costa Rica is what I would do.

Real Angie   Money would probably fix like 83 percent of it honestly. I'd take a fuck load of money. Can you write it for me?

Angie   The book? Fuck yeah. I got you. We'll give it a one word insta-hope title like: *Resilient* or *Irrepressible* or something. They'll make a movie, it'll be stupid, but someone will get an Oscar for it.

Real Angie   Great. Love it. Deal. You write it, I take credit.

Angie   Who would know.

Real Angie   I don't know, my mom seems to like you, which makes me think you're not doing a very good job of being me.

Angie   Fuck off. She enjoys my texts.

Real Angie   Exactly, but whatever you're doing is working for her and letting me off the hook, so keep that shit up, OK.

Angie   Sure thing. Done. Write a bestseller, text your mom, anything else?

Real Angie   Just like maybe we like, just talk to me about . . . me?

Angie   Yeah. We can talk anytime you want. But like also maybe get a dog.

Real Angie   Fuck off.

Angie   Or a cat, cats are cuddly bitches like us. Or we could like Build-a-Bear that shit? You know, those teddy bears with the voicebox? Your sister could rig that up I bet.

Real Angie   Oh my god what if I put you in my Care Bear from when I was a kid! I know Mere has it somewhere.

Angie   The pink one with the rainbow?

Real Angie   Cheer Bear!

Angie   Oh I love Cheer Bear!

Real Angie   Girl I'm saying you could *be* Cheer Bear.

Angie   Ooooooooooh, that is some serious manifesting and I am *into it*.

(*Pause. The real question she wants to ask.*)

Real Angie   Why didn't you tell her about those messages?

(**Merril** *is stunned. What the fuck did she just say?*)

. . .

From him? I read them two years ago and like never responded because what the fuck, right?

But you had to have known they were there. Right there.

I don't know how you work but . . .

You had *all* my information.

Why did you wait to tell her?

Why did you wait to come get me?

Silence. **Merril** *cannot believe this. Did* **Angie** *really know from the start?*

Angie   I was protecting your sister.

Merril   What?

Real Angie   From me?

Protecting *her* from *me?*

   Merril   NO.

      Angie   Yes.

         Merril   NO.

Angie   She loved you more than anything.

But it's usually someone you love. Who hurts you most.

Merril   Hey. No –

   Angie   And she didn't design me to get you back, she designed me for . . . closure.

      Real Angie   'People need reminding of what they actually want.'

         Angie   Yes.

            Real Angie   And she didn't actually want me?

               Merril   NoNoNo hey that's not true, that's not at all true, Angie –

                  Real Angie   LET HER TALK.

                     Merril   Angie, stop this, Angie.

                        Real Angie   WHICH ONE?

Merril   OK.

I need to explain what it's saying –

Real Angie   It's saying that you made a sister you like better than me.

Merril   That's not true, not better, that's not what I was doing,

Real Angie   Seems exactly what you were doing –

Merril   No it's not, there *are* differences, but it was subconscious –

Real Angie   Bullshit –

Merril   Angie listen to me –

Real Angie   NoNoNo I get it, better would have been nice. I wanted better too, I wanted a very very different, better world because he came for *ME* – OK – everyday he came for *ME*, and I'm sitting there thinking 'They're coming! They'll come for me,' and no. No one was coming. No one was coming because no one wanted me back.

Merril   That's not true. We couldn't find you!

Real Angie   BULLSHIT, NO ONE SAVES A FUCKING NIGHTMARE.

(*Breathing hard, fast, upset again, thinking of it all again, fuck fuck fuck.*

Real Angie *just starts to cry, heave, rage, wail, break shit, whatever trauma looks like in her this is it – it's rolling.*)

Merril HeyHey, you need	**Angie** Just breath, Angie.
to breathe, OK.	Breathe.
If you're having a panic	I understand how hard this is.
attack you need	*I'm here.*
to try and breathe.	
Don't listen to that shit,	
that's not real,	
I'm here –	

Real Angie   GET THE FUCK AWAY FROM ME.

Merril   Angie.

Real Angie   *ITS. FUCKING. AGONY IN HERE.*

    Merril   *Angie stop –*

| **Real Angie**   *NO NO NO WHY DIDN'T YOU JUST LEAVE ME, YOU DON'T WANT ME, YOU DON'T, YOU DON'T, NO ONE DOES, SHE DIDN'T AND YOU DON'T, AND HE WAS – HE WAS – HE WAS THE ONLY ONE WHO CHOSE ME.* | **Merril**   Angie. Ange, come on. Hey, stop, listen – Angie, stop. *Angie –* |

Merril (*snaps back at her hard*)   *UH UH, NO YOU FUCKING DON'T, I WAS THE ONE WHO CHOSE YOU, I WILL ALWAYS CHOOSE YOU.*

(**Angie** *does, still shaking, can't be touched.*)

Angie (*voice*)   Hold on, Angie, please hold on –

Merril (*to the program*)   STOP.

Angie (*voice*)   I'm trying to help her –

Merril (*to the program*)   SHUT DOWN, ANGIE STOP, *STOP.*

(**Angie** *stops.*

Merril *might slam the laptop shut, and goes back to* **Real Angie**.)

Merril   I'm sorry. I'm – I'm – I didn't – I'm sorry. She has nothing to do with you.

(**Real Angie** *lets out a small laugh at the absurdity of this.*

Merril *tries to touch her,* **Real Angie** *pushes her off again.*

Merril *takes the hint and sits near her, but not right next to her.*

Silence. Doesn't know what to say. Says what she does know.)

Merril The Turing Test is famous, right, it was supposed to measure artificial intelligence, basically a program passes if it convinces humans it's human.

Real Angie I don't fucking care –

Merril I know, shut up, I love you –

And OK, the Turing test was passed a while ago, but because human judges would interact with other humans as well as computers to be able to compare them, there were two awards they would give out. An award for the 'most human computer' and one for the 'Most Human Human.'

Real Angie That's literally the dumbest.

Merril I know. Because every human is the most human. Every one.

You are unreplicable. No one can be remade, that's the beautiful tragedy of it all.

This thing did its job, but it's not you, and I want *you, I have always wanted you.*

You. Are. Wanted.

My Most Human Sister is a Wonder of the Fucking World.

(*Pause.*)

Real Angie I don't know. You should probably keep the other one. She'll last longer.

Merril Hey.

Real Angie I want to die.

Merril *Hey.*

Real Angie But I do I do, I don't think I can do this –

Merril *Yes you can.* My unstoppable sister. You are resilience, you are survival, you are the most human human because you are the one that fucking lives. And I have no idea how we're gonna get through this or past this except that we will. You bet we fucking will. We will build the path by walking, and we will walk together. You and me, is the pattern. I love you, is the pattern, I'm not leaving, is the pattern. I keep going because you keep going. And going is so much the pattern of you that the AI knew it the second I turned it on. Somehow it knew nothing would stop you. So, you're not going to stop. You couldn't if you tried. You will keep going. And going and going.

(*She's doing what she said: 'I'm here, I'm not leaving.'*

Suddenly **Real Angie** *grabs* **Merril***'s hand. Weeping or trying not to.*

She needs her sister so badly, but this might be all she can manage today.

Merril *accepts this, squeezes her hand back.*)

Real Angie   Thank you.

(**Merril** *might help her sister to her feet. They might finally exit the space together.*

Or they might just sit together and embrace in a big way.

Or they might just sit for a moment or two until . . .)

Angie   Thank you.

(*Black out.*)

The End.